The Whole Bible
Points to Jesus

HOLLY DESVIGNES

WESTBOW
PRESS®
A DIVISION OF THOMAS NELSON
& ZONDERVAN

WestBow Press books may be ordered through booksellers or by contacting:

WestBow Press
A Division of Thomas Nelson & Zondervan
1663 Liberty Drive
Bloomington, IN 47403
www.westbowpress.com
844-714-3454

ISBN: 978-1-6642-0502-4 (sc)
ISBN: 978-1-6642-0503-1 (e)

Library of Congress Control Number: 2020917432

Print information available on the last page.

WestBow Press rev. date: 10/08/2020

INTRODUCTION

Many people do not understand that the Bible is one book, connected by one theme, which is Jesus Christ coming to be the Savior of the world.

The Whole Bible Points to Jesus is an informational activity book that teaches how and where Jesus is found in the whole Bible. There are activities to help illustrate this truth, as well as challenges that are a bit more difficult to solve. Everything is designed to teach that Jesus is the central theme of the entire Bible from beginning to end.

TWO PARTS OF THE BIBLE

The Bible is divided into two parts:

The first part is called the Old Testament, and the second part is called the New Testament.

Activity

Which part tells us about Jesus?

- Circle where we can find Jesus:

- The Old Testament

- The New Testament

- Both

If you circled the Old Testament, you were right.
If you circled the New Testament, you were right.
If you circled both, you were right!

How can that be true?

It's true because the whole Bible is about Jesus. The Old Testament and New Testament are connected by telling the same story, the story of Jesus.

Many people have learned that the Bible consists of sixty-six books, written by various authors during different periods of time. It is, but it is also one book, written by one author, God, with one theme, that Jesus is the Savior.

THE MESSAGE OF THE OLD TESTAMENT

The Old Testament tells us:

"The Savior is coming!"

Activity

Draw an arrow in red pointing to the right.

THE MESSAGE OF THE NEW TESTAMENT

The New Testament tells us:

"The Savior is here!"

CLUES

God has placed clues throughout the Old Testament to tell us about who Jesus is, what He's like and what He's coming to do for us.

There are three different types of clues in the Old Testament.

1. Prophecy
2. Picture
3. Preincarnate Appearance

PROPHECY

This is the first type of clue in the Old Testament.

Activity

Can you make a "P" look like it's proclaiming a message?

A prophecy tells us something that is to come, or, in other words, the future. There are many prophecies about Jesus, God's Son and our Savior, coming. The first is in Genesis 3:15, where God curses the serpent after Adam and Eve ate the forbidden fruit. It says, "And I will cause hostility between you and the woman, and between your offspring and her offspring. He will strike (or crush) your head and you will strike (or bruise) His heel."

This verse is not about women being afraid of snakes! Satan influenced the serpent, so God is really speaking to him. The woman's offspring looks ahead to Jesus, born to Mary through God's Spirit. Satan and Jesus are on opposite sides in this spiritual war, and, although Satan wounds Jesus on the cross, Jesus death for our sins on that cross crushes Satan and defeats him forever.

Challenge

Can you find another prophecy about Jesus in the Old Testament? (Hint: There are some in later books, and many are about His birth or death.) What do you learn about Him from this prophecy?

PICTURE

This is the second type of clue in the Old Testament.

Activity

Can you turn a "P" into a picture of Jesus?

Pictures are God's illustrations of Jesus, His Son and our Savior. They describe what Jesus is like and what He would do for us. The ark that Noah built in Genesis 6: 9-22 is the first picture of Jesus. Peter refers to this in I Peter 3: 19-21. The world was very evil, and everyone (except Noah, his wife, his three sons and their wives) refused to obey God. The flood was God's punishment for their sin. Noah and his family were saved from the flood's punishment when they entered the ark by faith. When we believe in Jesus by faith, we are saved from God's eternal punishment for sin.

Challenge

Can you find another picture of Jesus in Genesis? (Hint: It also involves a father, a son and a sacrifice.)

What does this tell us about Jesus?

PREINCARNATE APPEARANCE

This is the third type of clue in the Old Testament.

Activity

Can you make this "P" look like a king?

Preincarnate is a big word, but it simply means, "before having a body." These are appearances of Jesus before He was born on earth in Bethlehem. Jesus is God, the Son, so He has always existed. He had no beginning and has no end, for He is eternal. He came into our world as a baby when He was born to Mary in Bethlehem. He had a real human body for thirty-three years, up until He died on the cross. During these years He was fully human as well as fully God. However, He always existed as God! We see Him in the Old Testament. Sometimes He temporarily assumed a body. Sometimes He appeared as "the Angel of the Lord" (not an angel, but the Angel). The first mention of the Angel of the Lord is in Genesis 16:7, where He meets Hagar, the Egyptian servant of Abraham's wife, Sarah. Hagar calls Him "the God who sees me." (Genesis 16:13). The first mention of Jesus appearing as a man is to Abraham in Genesis 18, where He comes by Abraham's tent as a traveler. This person could foretell the future, read Sarah's mind and control the coming judgment of Sodom and Gomorrah.

Challenge

Can you find another mention of the Angel of the Lord or another time Jesus appeared to someone in the Old Testament?

GENESIS

What Begins in Genesis

The story of Jesus starts in the first book of the Bible, Genesis, which means "beginning." A lot starts in Genesis, actually!

Creation of the universe is the first thing that begins in Genesis. This is probably what most people think of when Genesis is mentioned. God created all we see, hear and touch in six days. In the first five days He made the sun, moon, stars and all the plants and animals.

Activity

Draw a picture of your favorite created thing.

GENESIS

The Sixth Day of Creation

On the sixth day of creation, God created something different, something unique! He created people. People are different from the rest of creation because they were created "in God's image" (Genesis 1:27). What does that mean? One thing it means is that people were created to have a relationship with God, know Him, love Him, obey or (in Adam and Eve's case) disobey Him.

As much as we love our pets, or animals in general, they cannot know God. They can't pray, read His Word, know His love or seek Him. God walked with Adam "in the cool of the day" (Genesis 3:8), not with a giraffe, an elephant, a lion, or even a chimpanzee. People were made to have an eternal relationship with God. We were designed to live forever with Him, but something happened that came between us and God. Uh oh…

Activity

Glue or tape a picture of yourself below.

GENESIS

The Second Thing that Begins in Genesis

Sin is the second thing that begins in Genesis.

The first man and woman, Adam and Eve, disobeyed God's command not to eat from the tree of the knowledge of good and evil. They could eat from every other tree, but not that one. Eve was tempted and gave in, then Adam ate, too. This disobedience is called sin, and every person born since has inherited that sin nature from them. It's part of being human. This is the reason why everyone dies. God said they would die if they sinned, and they did. Every person who is born also dies because everyone is a sinner. We were born with a sin nature, inherited from Adam, and we also commit sin. "The soul that sins will die," it says in Ezekiel 18:20 (in the Old Testament) and "the wages of sin is death," Paul writes in Romans 6:23 (in the New Testament). We all sin, and therefore fall short of the glory of God" (Romans 3:23).

So far, we've learned that God created people in His image, in order to have an eternal relationship with Him. However, people have a problem, called sin, that brings death and eternal separation from God. We need help! We need a Savior!

AN ILLUSTRATION OF SIN

Before Adam and Eve sinned, they walked in close fellowship with God. There was no separation.

Activity

This page of paper has no separation in it…yet. Cut a vertical line from the bottom of the page up to point A.

Draw a horizontal line from point B to point C. Write "God" on this horizontal line to the right of the vertical line and write "man" on the horizontal line to the left of the vertical line.

This illustrates how we are separated from God by our sin.

A

B   C

GENESIS

The Third Thing that Begins in Genesis

God's chosen people, the Israelites, is the third thing that begins in Genesis.

God made all people special, but He chose to reveal Himself in a deeper way to a certain group, the Israelites, or Jews. They, in turn, were to show the world what God was like – His nature and His laws. Very importantly, the promised Savior, Jesus Christ, was to come in His human form from these people. In Genesis 12, God calls Abram (later to be renamed Abraham) to leave his home and go to a land God would show him. He didn't have GPS, or even a map, but he and his family picked up and left, God guiding him. God brought him to the promised land, the land of Israel (it was called Canaan at the time). God made several promises to Abram. One was that He'd make him into a great nation. A second promise was that Abram would be a blessing to all peoples of the earth (a prophecy about the coming Savior, Jesus). A third promise was that this land would belong to Abram's descendants forever.

This is where Jesus' earthly family tree starts, with Abram, or Abraham, as God later renamed him.

JESUS' FAMILY TREE

Here is a partial overview of Jesus' family tree:

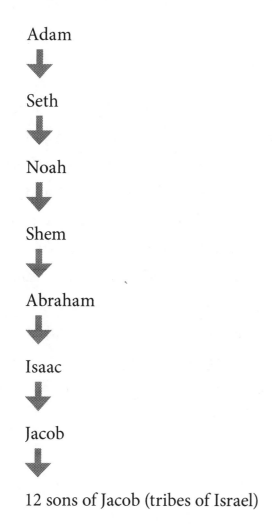

Adam

Seth

Noah

Shem

Abraham

Isaac

Jacob

12 sons of Jacob (tribes of Israel)

One of Jacob's sons was named Judah. King David was a descendant of Judah, and Jesus came through David's line.

This is Jesus' human, or earthly, family tree. But why exactly did He come to earth?

LET'S REVIEW

The fourth thing that begins in Genesis is a very important concept and explains the reason Jesus came to earth.

First, let's review what we've learned so far.

God created everything. On the final or sixth day He created people, different from everything else because they were created in His image, able to have a relationship with Him, know Him, love Him, obey or disobey Him. The first two people, Adam and Eve, disobeyed and did something God had told them not to do. Since all people are descended from Adam and Eve, every person has inherited a sin nature from them. Everyone is a sinner. We have a problem! We were made to have a close relationship with God, but our sin has separated us from Him. He loves us, but He is holy, or completely pure, so no sin can come into His presence. God always has a plan, and He designed one for this situation. He's going to send someone, His only Son, Jesus, to save us from our sins. Jesus is God, but He also became a man, an Israelite, from the tribe of Judah and the line of David. How is He going to save us? That's where the fourth thing that started in Genesis comes into the picture.

GENESIS

The Fourth Thing that Begins in Genesis

The substitution principle is the fourth thing that begins in Genesis.

What is the substitution principle?

It means that the innocent becomes a substitute for the guilty. The innocent takes the place of the guilty and pays the price of their sin.

Imagine a judge pronouncing someone guilty for a crime, and they are truly guilty. Then the judge's son comes in and says he'll take the guilty person's punishment. The judge agrees, so the guilty person goes free, while the judge's son is condemned.

In the Old Testament God set up a sacrificial system as part of His law, given to the Israelites. (This system started even before the law was given, actually.) In that system innocent animals took the place of guilty sinners, bearing the penalty of death, and the guilty person was forgiven.

In the New Testament God fulfilled this sacrificial system as Jesus became the ultimate substitute, the Lamb of God, whose sacrificial death and shed blood has the power to cleanse and remove everyone's sin. We are all guilty sinners, deserving of death, but when we put our faith in our substitute and believe He took our place and bore our punishment, we are forgiven!

THE TWO SACRIFICIAL SYSTEMS

Activity

The Old Testament Sacrificial System

INNOCENT

Draw an animal (sheep, goat, calf, etc.)

GUILTY

Draw a person who's forgiven

| | |
| | |

The New Testament Sacrificial System

INNOCENT

Draw the Cross

GUILTY

Draw people who are forgiven

| | |
| | |

The Old Testament foreshadows, or points to, the ultimate sacrifice in the New Testament, Jesus Christ. The animal sacrifices in the Old Testament were not a final solution since they had to be repeated over and over. People sin more than once! Animals were only a temporary fix. Jesus' sacrifice, though, was once for all, never to be repeated, because it, and He, is perfect! Jesus was sinless, as God is, so His death solved everyone's sin problem. Every person's sins, all of them, are forgiven forever the moment that person believes in Jesus as his or her Savior and perfect substitute.

SUMMING IT UP

Problem: God loves people and wants to have a relationship with them. People are sinners. Since God is holy, He cannot allow sin in His presence.

Solution: God provides a way for people's sins to be forgiven. In the Old Testament worshipers offered a sacrifice of an innocent animal by faith. God accepted this offering as a temporary substitute for the worshiper and forgave his sin. In the New Testament people must believe that Jesus is the final substitute God provided to die in their place. When they believe this, they are forgiven of all their sins.

Activity

Turn back to the page you cut. Make a cross out of red paper. (You can color the paper red if you only have white.) Make the center, vertical post about as long as the cut you made on that page. Make the horizontal crossbeam so it will fit under the words "God" and "man" as closely as you can. (If the crossbeam covers the words, you can write them above or on it instead). The cross of Jesus Christ connects God and man, and we can have that relationship with Him that we were meant to have. The cross restores our relationship to God. It is the only thing that can since we can do nothing by ourselves to wipe away our sins. Only faith in Jesus as our substitute will do that.

AFTER GENESIS

Remember, Genesis is the first book of the Bible, and it means "beginning." A lot begins in Genesis! We covered four things: creation, sin, God's chosen people and the substitution principle. This is where the whole foundation of our salvation begins.

The rest of the Old Testament is the history of the Israelites, God's chosen people, through whom Jesus, our Savior, came. It tells us what happened to them, and the land of Israel, up until 400 years before Jesus' birth in Bethlehem.

EXODUS

The second book is Exodus, which means "going out"" (like exit).

Who went out and from where?

The Israelites went out from Egypt. God used Moses to lead them out.

How did they get into Egypt?

That story begins at the end of Genesis. Abraham's son, Isaac, had two sons. One was named Jacob. Jacob had twelve sons, which became the twelve tribes of Israel. One of Jacob's youngest sons, Joseph, was sold to some slave traders by his own brothers, who were jealous of him. He ended up as a slave in Egypt. God gave him the ability to interpret dreams, and when he interpreted a dream that the Egyptian king, Pharaoh, had, he was promoted to second-in-command! Pharaoh's dream had predicted a world-wide famine, and when that came to pass, Egypt was prepared and had plenty of food stored away, thanks to Joseph's planning. People from other countries came to Egypt to buy food there, and Joseph's brothers eventually came, too. He forgave them and had them bring his father and all his family (about 70 people) to Egypt, where he supported them. They lived there for over 400 years, but, unfortunately, became enslaved by the Egyptians.

Now Moses comes into the picture, at the beginning of Exodus, and God uses him to deliver the Israelites from slavery in Egypt.

LEVITICUS

The third book is Leviticus, which tells us about the law of God, including all the feasts, sacrifices and other actions involved in obeying the law. It emphasizes the holiness of God.

The book is named after Levi, another son of Jacob, which was the tribe that became priests and Levites, those who served the Lord in the Temple.

So, Leviticus is "the law."

NUMBERS

The fourth book is Numbers.

The best way to sum up this book is the word "rebellion."

It's given the name, Numbers, because the Israelites are counted by families at beginning of the book. However, rebellion is the singular characteristic of the Israelites throughout this book. Their biggest rebellion is refusing to enter the land God promised to give them (in chapters 13 and 14). Moses brought them right to the edge of the land, but because they were afraid of the people who lived there, they wouldn't enter it. They didn't trust the Lord! God punished them by making them continue to wander in the desert for forty years. They couldn't go in, but God said their children would.

DEUTERONOMY

The fifth book is Deuteronomy. It's a long, hard name to pronounce, but it simply means "the second giving of the law." The root of this big word means "two", like duet, duo, or even double.

Why did the law need to be given again? In the forty years that the Israelites wandered around the desert because they refused to go into the land God promised them, all the adults died. Their children did not, however. God was going to bring this next generation into the land, so they needed to hear the law again.

THE PENTATEUCH

These first five books of the Bible are called the Pentateuch. "Penta" means five (like a five-sided figure, or pentagon.) "Teuch" means books or writings. They were written by Moses and tell the early history of Israel, plus the spelling out of the law. Many, many important things begin in the Pentateuch, things that help us understand the New Testament and Jesus' coming.

Challenge

Find one example of each "P" clue in the other four books of the Pentateuch (not Genesis).

THE HISTORICAL BOOKS

The next twelve books in the Old Testament (Joshua through Esther) are called the Historical Books. They tell of Israel's next historical step, entering the promised land. They tell of the Israelites' lives there, then end with their exile from the land when God expels them from it because of their sin. They then are taken into captivity to foreign lands. This is called the Exile.

JOSHUA

Joshua, which follows Deuteronomy, is best described with the words "going in." The children of those who refused to go into the promised land are led into that land by Joshua. Moses had died at the end of Genesis, and Joshua was his second-in-command. God appoints Joshua to lead His people into the land He's giving them. And they go in!

JUDGES

Judges can be summed up "judges rule!"

The Israelites are in their land, but they are very loosely connected at this point. The land has been divided up, according to each tribe. However, everyone "does as he sees fit" (Judges 21:25), and not many obey the Lord.

In fact, there's a cycle in Judges that's repeated over and over, round and round like a bicycle wheel. The people disobey; God sends a foreign nation to oppress them; they cry out to God; He sends a judge, or deliverer; they obey while the judge is ruling. Then it starts all over when they disobey again.

It's a circle like this:

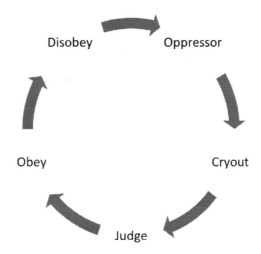

Disobey → Oppressor → Cryout → Judge → Obey

Challenge

Can you find the name of one oppressor of Israel and the judge who delivered them, then make your own circle?

RUTH

Ruth is a beautiful story that takes place during the time of the judges.

Remember that "not many" obeyed the Lord during that time? A few did, though. This is a story about some who did. It is an amazing story of God's provision and guidance, and it also reveals a piece of Jesus' ancestry!

Challenge

Can you find the names of some of Jesus' ancestors in Ruth?

---

1 AND 2 SAMUEL

1 and 2 Samuel were originally just one book in the Hebrew Scriptures (what we now call the Old Testament). A word that describes these books is "transition." The Israelite nation transitioned from local judges to national kings. These books tell the story of Samuel, the last judge of Israel, who was also a prophet, and of the Israelites' desire for a king. Samuel first anoints Saul as king, who disobeys the Lord. The Lord then tells Samuel to anoint David, who eventually becomes king and reigns for forty years. 2 Samuel concludes with a very elderly king David near the end of his reign.

1 AND 2 KINGS

These books (also one in the Hebrew Scripture) and 1 and 2 Chronicles (again, one book) tell about the progression of the kings in Israel. So, all of them mean "kings rule!"

1 and 2 Kings start with the end of David's reign, move through the Golden Age of Solomon (David's son) and recount the split of the nation into two parts. The northern kingdom was called Israel, and the southern kingdom was named Judah. They end with the collapse of the whole nation, and everyone being taken from their land into exile in foreign countries. Israel was taken to Assyria, and a bit later Judah to Babylon.

1 AND 2 CHRONICLES

1 and 2 Chronicles cover the same time frame, with an introduction of the genealogies of the twelve sons of Jacob in the first nine chapters of 1 Chronicles. These books then move from David's reign to the fall of Jerusalem in Judah to Babylon.

EZRA AND NEHEMIAH

The word that sums up both these books is "rebuilding." God promised that the Israelites would go home, back to their land, after seventy years, and they did. Ezra focuses on rebuilding the Temple, while Nehemiah focuses on rebuilding the walls of Jerusalem.

It was never quite the same as it used to be, though.

ESTHER

Esther, like Ruth, is a story that takes place within another timeframe. Ruth took place during the period of the judges, while Esther is set in the time of Israel's exile. This time of exile was extremely hard on the Jewish people, and this is an encouraging and amazing story of how one woman saved her people from extinction.

This ends the Historical Books of the Old Testament.

Challenge

Can you find where it says Jesus will sit on the throne of David? (clue: It says David's throne will be established forever, and it's in one of the "kings rule" books.)

THE WISDOM BOOKS

The next five books, Job through the Song of Songs, do not advance the history of Israel. They were written during different points in their history.

JOB

The first of the Wisdom Books is Job. Job talks about "suffering". Job is a righteous man (God says so Himself), but he goes through terrible loss and suffering. His friends say that he's suffering because he'd sinned, but he hadn't. Many people believed that suffering is always caused by sin, and some still believe that today. Job challenges this theory. Sometimes we never know why we, or anyone else, suffer, but we still can trust God. He is in control and loves us!

PSALMS

The Psalms are actually "songs", and that's the word used to describe this book. It's the longest book in the Old Testament, with 150 psalms (or chapters.) Many were written by David both before and after he became king, but not all were. A man named Asaph wrote some, and even Moses wrote one. Many were used in worship, both in Old and New Testament times. All express deep emotions. There are prophecies and pictures about Jesus in the Psalms, as well.

Challenge

Can you find a psalm that tells us about Jesus' death?

PROVERBS

Proverbs is best known as the book of "wisdom." This book is mostly made up of wise short sayings that give readers guidance in words, actions and attitudes. Much of this book was written by Solomon.

Challenge

Can you find a proverb that people use as an expression today (some without knowing where it came from)?

ECCLESIASTES

Ecclesiastes is about the "meaningless of life" from the human perspective, which is what "under the sun" means. It was also written by Solomon. King Solomon was the wisest and richest man on earth, probably of all time. Towards the end of his life, he decided to try everything, like possessions, pleasure and power, to see what brought meaning to his life. His conclusion? Read chapter 12, verse 13 (the next to the last verse of the book) for the answer.

SONG OF SONGS

Song of Songs, or Song of Solomon, is a "love poem" also written by King Solomon. It describes the love between Solomon and his bride, as well as picturing the love between Jesus (the King of kings) and the church (His bride).

THE PROPHETS

The next section of books are the Prophets, and this group finishes the Old Testament. The books are divided into two groups: Major Prophets, which are not more important, just longer, and Minor Prophets, which are not less important, just shorter.

These books were written by God's prophets who prophesied at different periods of time, under the rule of different kings, some in the northern kingdom and some in the southern, throughout Israel's history. They do not advance Israel's history, just take place during events that have been already recorded.

Some of their prophecies were future to them but are now history to us. Some are still future to us and deal with things still to come when Jesus returns as angels told us in Acts 1:11.

ISAIAH

Isaiah prophesied in the southern kingdom, Judah, during the reigns of four kings: Uzziah, Jotham, Ahaz and Hezekiah. He probably died sometime during the reign of Hezekiah's son, Manasseh. This was between 740 and 680 B.C. (Before Christ)

Isaiah, along with all the other major (and minor) prophets, has the general theme of judgment of both northern and southern kingdoms for their sins, especially idolatry, and their eventual forgiveness and restoration. Isaiah can be summed up "judgment and comfort."

Challenge

Find the chapter that describes Jesus and His work for us on the cross.

JEREMIAH AND LAMENTATIONS

The prophet Jeremiah wrote the prophetic book that bears his name, as well as the book of Lamentations. He was a prophet in the southern kingdom before and then after it fell to the Babylonians. He was known as the "weeping prophet" because he grieved so much over the nation's sins and God's judgment.

Jeremiah can be summed up as "grief to joy." Lamentations is a "song of sorrow", a poem of mourning over chastisement of sin and the resulting exile.

EZEKIEL

Ezekiel is called an 'exilic' prophet since he lived among the Jewish exiles in Babylon and prophesied there. He had many unique visions and prophecies that told the people then, and us now, about God's plans for the future, many of which are still to come. It can be summarized by the terms "punishment, then restoration."

DANIEL

Daniel is a shorter book but is considered one of the major prophets because it contains some very important and detailed prophecies. Daniel was also an 'exilic' prophet, since he was taken to Babylon as a teenager and spent his whole life there, serving under several foreign kings. A good word to describe Daniel is "courage".

THE MINOR PROPHETS

The Minor Prophets are not minor in importance but are just smaller books in length. There are twelve of them, and their writers' ministries stretched over approximately 400 years, from the 9th to 5th century B.C. The prophets come from different backgrounds and prophesy to different kingdoms at different times. Their writing styles and prophecies differ, too, but they all tell of Israel's or Judah's sin, God's judgment on them and their eventual restoration. Sometimes judgment was pronounced on another country. Remember, some prophecies have been fulfilled already so are now history to us, and some are still to be fulfilled so are still in the future for us. Of course, when Jesus comes the second time, all prophecies will be fulfilled. There are prophecies that tell us about Jesus all through the Minor Prophets.

Challenge

Can you find which prophet tells us where Jesus would be born? (Name of book, chapter and verse)

Bonus Challenge

Can you name all twelve of the minor prophets in order? There is no set way to learn them. You can use a song or memorize the first initial of each book. Whatever works for you!

SILENCE

Next follow 400 years of silence from God! Between Malachi, the last book in the Old Testament, written about 400 B.C., to the birth of Jesus in Bethlehem, God was silent. There were no prophecies, no communication, nothing. Imagine reading a book and reaching 400 blank pages! Is the book over? This one isn't. God speaks loudly and clearly in the New Testament though Jesus, His Son and our Savior.

There are no more clues because Jesus is here! However, there is a mystery that is revealed in the New Testament. One Bible teacher calls it a (parenthesis). It's something no one in the Old Testament, even the prophets, saw coming.

Activity

Can you figure out this word search that tells us what the mystery is?

(Check horizontally, vertically and diagonally.)

D	C	M	R	E	G	C
S	T	H	A	S	H	E
C	B	H	B	U	T	D
H	S	A	R	M	P	E
E	G	C	D	U	Y	N
N	H	R	C	P	A	H

Hint: The first two letters are the last two letters, and you are in the middle!

THE GOSPELS

The first four books of the New Testament are called the Gospels, and they tell the story of Jesus' life here on earth as a man. He is also God, so remember He is both human and divine.

Each Gospel is a little different, telling both some different stories as well as some of the same events, but with different details. They don't contradict each other, just tell things about Jesus' life and ministry from a unique perspective and with a slightly different purpose. They all lay the foundation for the "mystery" to be revealed.

MATTHEW

Matthew is the first Gospel. It was written by Matthew, one of Jesus' twelve disciples, called apostles, who had been a tax collector. His perspective is "Jesus the King," the son of David. He starts with Jesus' genealogy, traced back King David, and also emphasizes Bethlehem, the home of David. He calls him "The Son of David" many times, and His kingdom is mentioned over fifty times. Matthew contains the most Old Testament prophecies fulfilled by Jesus.

Challenge

Can you find a fulfilled prophecy about Jesus in Matthew? Where is it found in the Old Testament?

MARK

Mark is the second Gospel. The author was John Mark, a nephew of Barnabas, a prominent missionary in the book of Acts, who traveled with Paul on his first missionary journey. He is thought to be a close friend of Jesus' disciple, Peter, and this Gospel reflects Peter's view and account of Jesus' life and ministry. His perspective is "Christ the Servant." Mark is the shortest Gospel and has a lot of action in its narrative. There is no genealogy, since one isn't usually needed for a servant. The emphasis is on Jesus as the Servant of the Lord, but Mark still presents Him as the powerful Son of God.

LUKE

Luke is the third Gospel. Some think Luke was a Gentile (non-Jew), but most scholars feel he was Jewish. He was a doctor, and he also wrote the book of Acts. He was a companion of Paul and accompanied him on some of his missionary journeys. Luke's perspective is Jesus as the "Son of Man," in His perfect humanity. Luke, like Matthew, contains a genealogy. Luke's traces Jesus' lineage back to Adam. Luke is the only one who tells a bit about Jesus' boyhood. He also emphasizes Jesus' prayer life, sympathy for those in need and believing women's ministry to Jesus.

These three Gospels (Matthew, Mark and Luke) are called the Synoptic Gospels. Synoptic comes from a Greek word meaning "together sight". There are many similarities between the three, but there are significant differences, too.

Challenge

Can you find an event or story that is in all three? Look carefully. What is the same? What is different?

JOHN

John is the fourth Gospel, written by John, one of Jesus' twelve disciples. It is quite different and contains many unique events and sayings not found in the other gospels. John gives the perspective of Jesus being the "Son of God," or as Deity. Remember, He was 100% human and 100% God at the same time! There is no genealogy because God has always existed. He is the only gospel writer that gives Jesus the title "the Word". The first verses make it plain that He was from the beginning, was God, created all things and is both life and light. John is the only one who records the eight "I am" declarations that Jesus called Himself, including the one that God told Moses, simply "I Am" (Exodus 3:14).

Challenge

Can you find all the "I Am" statements that Jesus made about Himself and where they are found in John? List them underneath.

REVIEW

Let's review for a moment.

In Genesis we learned that:

- God created the world, including people
- People sinned (disobeyed God)
- God had a plan to save them from the penalty of sin, death, right from the beginning
- He is going to send a Savior to save people from this penalty

In the rest of the Old Testament we see clues about God's plan:

- God chose a special people, the Israelites, through whom the Savior would come, humanly speaking.
- This Savior would also be God's Son, so He'd be both a human being and God.
- He is the perfect substitute, or sacrifice, to pay the penalty for people's sins.

The Old Testament also traces the history of the Israelite people, up to their exile from the promised land God had given them.

Then God is silent for approximately 400 years, after the last book of the Old Testament, until He speaks in the New Testament when Jesus is born.

The four Gospels (the first four books of the New Testament) tell about His birth, life, death and resurrection.

The Savior had come and completed God's plan for the salvation of the whole world!

ACTS

The book of Acts follows the gospels, and it is the only historical book in the New Testament. It was written by Luke, the author of the gospel bearing his name, and it tells of the development and growth of the church. A quick way to sum up Acts is "the early church".

At the very beginning of the book Jesus returns to Heaven, with a promise to return. God's Holy Spirit comes upon and empowers Jesus' disciples, and the church begins, then grows. Through the missionary journeys of Paul and others, Christianity spreads across the known world and churches are planted. Both Jews and Gentiles become Christians and meet in homes, since there were no church buildings until about the 3rd century A.D. The book ends with Paul telling everyone the gospel message from a prison in Rome. He wrote some of his letters to various churches from there, as well.

Challenge

Can you find the name of a city mentioned in Acts where Paul sent a letter?

EPISTLES

The rest of the New Testament books, except for the last one, Revelation, are called "epistles". Epistles are letters, many written by Paul, sent to strengthen, encourage and teach young Christians and guide fledgling churches. They were also meant to instruct the church throughout the ages.

ROMANS

The first letter is Romans, written by Paul to the church in Rome while he was in the city of Corinth. At this point Paul had not been to Rome, so he made sure that the Roman church received extensive teaching covering just about all the central truths of Christianity. It teaches about salvation, the role of faith, our relationship to Christ, the work of the Holy Spirit in our lives, God's sovereignty and how to live out our Christian faith in daily life. A lot is packed into its sixteen chapters!

Challenge

Can you find the "Romans Road" of salvations? Look up these verses: Romans 3:23, 6:23 and 10:9-10. What are the three points Paul makes here?

How would you explain salvation to someone using these verses?

1 AND 2 CORINTHIANS

1 and 2 Corinthians were letters written by Paul to the church in Corinth which he founded (the story of that is recorded in Acts 18). These letters, like some others, address certain problems in the church. In Paul's corrections of errors in their behavior or false teaching, we today also learn much truth, because their problems were not much different from ours. They lived in a city known for its sinful ways, similar to our society today, and struggled to live in a Christlike manner.

A good description of these letters is "Christian conduct in an ungodly culture."

GALATIANS

Galatians is a letter written by Paul to a group of churches in the region of Galatia (the country of Turkey today). He had visited Galatia and started some churches there during his first and third missionary journeys. Some letters were written to not just one but several churches and were meant to be passed around.

This letter was written to refute the false teaching that a person must obey a set of rules to be saved, which is called legalism.

A good description for Galatians is "liberty in Christ".

PRISON EPISTLES

The next three books, Ephesians, Philippians and Colossians, are most of Paul's prison epistles which were written while Paul was imprisoned in Rome.

EPHESIANS

Ephesians is another letter, like Galatians, that was written to a group of churches, not just to Ephesus, and was meant to be passed around among them. This letter tells us what the New Testament "mystery" is (check back to the page headed Silence). A Biblical mystery is something that hasn't been previously revealed, so no one has any idea what it is. Paul defines a mystery in Ephesians 3:3-5, then tells us plainly in 3:6 that this mystery is the church, the body of Jesus Christ, formed of Jews and Gentiles together with no distinction. We are all made one, saved by faith in Jesus Christ. No Old Testament prophet knew of this. The church is a brand-new creation, revealed and explained in detail here in Ephesians. Ephesians could be summarized "mystery revealed."

PHILIPPIANS

Philippians is a letter written to the church in Philippi, founded by Paul on his second missionary journey. Its theme is "joy", and it is a wonderful, encouraging example of how we can have joy in the midst of difficulty, like being in prison.

> ## Challenge
>
> Can you find where the church in Philippi was started in the book of Acts?

COLOSSIANS

Colossians was written by Paul to a church he hadn't started or even visited. It might have been founded by one of Paul's co-workers, Epaphras. Some false teachers had come into the church, and Paul had to correct their false teaching. A good summary for this letter would be "the supremacy of Christ," for He is supreme over everything!

1 AND 2 THESSALONIANS

1 and 2 Thessalonians were written by Paul to the church in Thessalonica which he founded on his second missionary journey. They were written from Corinth, not long after he left Thessalonica. Both letters deal with the return of Jesus Christ and events leading up to it. He is also correcting errors that false teachers had been telling them. These letters can be summed up as "Christ's return."

Challenge

Can you find in Acts where Paul started the church in Thessalonica? What happened there?

---

1 AND 2 TIMOTHY

1 and 2 Timothy were written by Paul, but not to a church. They were written to a person, Timothy, who was very close to Paul, his "his true son in faith." (1 Timothy 1:2). He was also one of Paul's companions on his second missionary journey. These letters, along with Titus, are called pastoral epistles, because these men were elders, or pastors, of churches. Since the church was a new institution, guidelines had to be established as to organization, leadership and discipline. Teaching needed to be sound, as well. God is a God of order, and this orderliness was to be reflected in the church. Even though most of us aren't pastors, or won't grow up to be, these epistles contain much good teaching for everyone! The best words for these epistles are "church order."

TITUS

Titus is also a pastoral epistle, written to another one of Paul's co-workers. The Bible never says how Titus and Paul met, but he and Paul were close, and they traveled together on Paul's third missionary journey. Titus ministered as a pastor in Crete, after he and Paul evangelized there. The letter instructs how leadership should be set up in the church and also emphasizes sound teaching. "Church order" sums up this epistle, as it does 1 and 2 Timothy.

PHILEMON

Philemon was also a letter Paul wrote while he was in prison in Rome (like Ephesians, Philippians and Colossians). It was written to a man who lived in the city of Colossae and whom Paul had led to faith in Christ. It deals with a specific situation but teaches all of us about true Christian love. A good summation of Philemon would be "oneness in Christ."

HEBREWS

Hebrews is a different kind of a book. It is a letter, but the writer is not identified, although many feel it is Paul. It is not addressed to a particular church or a person, either, but is written generally to new, and somewhat immature, Jewish believers scattered in different places. It teaches about who Christ is, what He did for us and how He is the fulfillment of the Old Testament, or Covenant. Its theme can be summed up in the sentence, "Christ is better."

Challenge

Christ is better than…what? List below as many things as you can find.

JAMES

James is called a general epistle. The next six books, 1 and 2 Peter, 1, 2 and 3 John and Jude, are also general epistles. They are letters that are not addressed to any certain church (or group of churches) or individual. James is one of the earliest epistles and was written by Jesus' brother to all the Jewish believers that were scattered among various nations. It is very direct and straightforward in its teaching. Many compare its style and content to the Old Testament book of Proverbs. Some of the same topics are covered, such as speech, wisdom, trials and justice. A good description of the book is "maturing in the faith."

1 AND 2 PETER

1 and 2 Peter were written by Peter, one of Jesus' twelve disciples, to Jewish believers scattered over a large area. Peter was a missionary primarily to the Jews, while Paul ministered mostly to the Gentiles (non-Jews). Both men witnessed to and taught everyone, however! Peter's first epistle mainly deals with "Christian suffering." His second epistle can be summed up as "last days", since it teaches a lot about the second coming of Christ.

Challenge

Can you find where Noah is mentioned in 2 Peter?

1, 2 AND 3 JOHN

1, 2, and 3 John were written by John, Jesus' disciple, as were the gospel and the Bible's final book, Revelation. They were all written late in John's life, years after he had written the gospel. 1 John was written to Christians in general and emphasizes "love and fellowship." As he got older, John was known as the apostle of love. 2 and 3 John are both very brief. 2 John is written to "the chosen lady and her children," so it could be to a person or church. 3 John is written to "his dear friend, Gaius." They both emphasize love and also warn against false teachers.

JUDE

Jude was written by another brother of Jesus, again to Christians in general. He started the letter with one purpose, to write about the salvation they shared, but because of dangerous false teachers, he changed his theme to "defending the faith." That's called apologetics, which is knowing what you believe and why you believe it. Stand up for God's truth!

REVELATION

The last book of the Bible is Revelation. It was written by John near the end of his life (he was probably in his 80's or, possibly, 90's). He had been exiled to the island of Patmos, which was a small, rocky, barren island used as a place where the Romans sent convicts as punishment. In John's case, he was being punished for preaching the gospel. Remember that Genesis meant "beginning"? Revelation is "ending". It's about the end of time, or as some call it, "the end times." Everyone is fascinated by mysterious future events, and there are many, many interpretations of what might happen during these end times, but one thing is certain: Jesus is coming back again! How can we know that? We know because He said He would (through angel messengers) in Acts 1:11.

BEGINNING AND ENDING

Below is a line that pictures eternity. The arrows on each end means it goes on into infinity both ways. It never begins, and it never ends. How then can Genesis be the "beginning" and Revelation the "ending"?

Activity

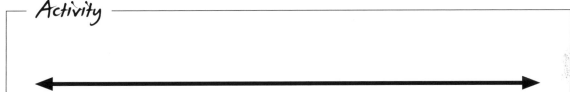

On the line above draw two dots about an inch apart. The space inside these two dots represents time. Time was also created by God. It began at creation and one day will end, when Jesus returns.

In that period called "time", God created the universe, the earth, you and me and everyone else. He dealt with the problem of sin, chose a special group of people through whom He revealed Himself and His law to the world, sent His Son to be the sacrifice for peoples' sins so they could be forgiven and restored to a right relationship with Him, established the church and sent out witnesses into the whole world. Finally, he will send His Son back to earth again to bring time to an end. That's quite a few things!

IT'S ALL ABOUT JESUS!

Remember, the story of the whole Bible is the story of Jesus. It's all about Him!

Jesus Himself said this when He was walking with two disciples on the road to the village of Emmaus. They were sad because Jesus had just been crucified and didn't realize their risen Lord was walking right next to them! As they walked, Jesus taught them all that was written about Him. In Luke 24:47 it says, "And beginning with Moses and all the prophets, He explained to them what was said in all the Scriptures concerning Himself." Also, when He appeared to His apostles, He said to them in Luke 24:44, "This is what I told you while I was still with you. Everything must be fulfilled that is written about Me in the law of Moses, the prophets and the Psalms." Luke 24:45 continues, "Then He opened their minds so they could understand the Scriptures."

So what part of the Bible tells us about Jesus? It all does!

HOW IS A PERSON SAVED?

It's very important that you understand how a person is saved!

Many people think we're saved by going to church, being baptized, being confirmed, going to Sunday School, walking down the aisle in a church service at a pastor's, or someone's, invitation to come forward, doing good things to help others or not doing too many seriously bad things.

Are we saved by any of these things? They are all good things, but they are not what saves us. What does then? Faith does. Saving faith is believing that Jesus died for us, that He took our place on the cross and paid the punishment we should have received, that is, spiritual death. Remember Romans 6:23? "The wages of sin is death." What we earn because we sin is death. However, Jesus took our place! He loved us and gave His life for us. The rest of Romans 6:23 says, "The gift of God is eternal life in Christ Jesus our Lord". It is a gift that we receive by faith. We cannot earn our salvation.

Then, when we are truly saved by faith, we do all those other things, such as get baptized, go to church, read the Bible, do good things and so on. We do those things because we are saved, not to earn our salvation!

HOW DOES A PERSON GROW AS A CHRISTIAN?

It's also very important that you understand how to grow as a Christian!

When someone trusts in Jesus as their personal Savior who died in their place, they are "born again," Jesus said in John 3:7. When a person is first born again, they are like spiritual babies. Babies need to grow! They aren't supposed to stay babies.

How does someone grow, or mature, spiritually?

First, in the same way that babies need milk, you must read the Bible (1 Peter 2:2). You should have your own study Bible that has notes, explanations, indexes and cross references (these give you other Bible verses that mention the same subject). You can underline verses or write down things God tells you in the margins. There are many good children's or youth study Bibles available. If you're not sure which is the right one for you, check with your parents, youth leader or pastor.

Second, as babies grow, they learn to talk. Talking to God is called prayer. Pray all the time (Paul says that in 1 Thessalonians 5:17). You don't need to use any special words, just talk to God as you would to anyone else, telling Him everything. He already knows it all anyway!

Third, spend time alone with God. That means no phone, computer or tablet, music or TV. There should be no distractions as you read His Word and talk to Him. Also, you need to listen to anything your heart tells you that He's saying to you. (Having a notebook to write things down is a good idea, too!)

Fourth, be baptized, go to church, attend Sunday School, youth group and take advantage of opportunities to serve others. Learn from other believers. Encourage them and be encouraged by them. Growing is a lifelong experience (Hebrews 10:25)!

Printed in the United States
By Bookmasters